MUSEUM PRESS CRAFTBOOKS

Edited by

John FitzMaurice Mills,

R.D.S., F.R.S.A.I., F.R.S.A.

STAINED GLASS

BY JAMES PATERSON,
A.R.C.A., N.R.D., A.M.G.P.

Museum Press Limited · London

First published in Great Britain by Museum Press Limited
39 Parker Street, London, W.C.2
1968

SBN: 273 48600 4

Filmset and Printed in Great Britain by
Bookprint Limited, Crawley, Sussex

CONTENTS

INTRODUCTION

The rich glow of colour so evident in the twelfth-century windows of the great Cathedral of Chartres is due to the combination and mixtures of colours which produce a mosaic quality of coloured light, vibrant and alive.

To appreciate this quality more fully an exercise in mosaic can be carried out using small pieces, preferably rectangles, of coloured glass. Before starting, decide upon a particular colour family, possibly green, in which there is a great variety. Then spend some time in cutting up a number of shapes. These rectangles can be squares, and long and narrow strips. Keep your squares small, within the range of half or three-quarters of an inch, as this initial exercise can be carried out just as completely and more cheaply than when working with larger pieces.

When the green pieces have been cut, take another sheet of glass with a contrasting colour—this could be ruby or purple— and cut out a further amount of shapes. Before beginning to arrange your mosaic you will need a large piece of plate glass, approximately 20 inches square. This should be thoroughly cleaned on both sides and laid down upon a sheet of white paper to allow one to observe the coloured glass more easily. If a light-table is available (Illustration 1); this will be far more satisfactory. It will be simpler to gauge the true impression of strength and quality of your coloured pieces, particularly in the case of dark tones, which when laid upon white paper will appear black.

A clear adhesive will be required and this can be either gum arabic or Bostik. The former is useful when one requires to dismember a completed exercise. All that has to be done is to pour hot water over the surface and the

1 Light-table, for cutting, painting and arranging dark coloured glass.

7

gum will soon dissolve to permit easy removal of the glass pieces, which can be used again. Select and place the rectangles down on the plate glass, the underside having been smeared with adhesive, and using your own discretion arrange a design. You will discover that similar colours placed closely together will appear weak in the final viewing compared to those placed at varying distances from each other. To complete the exercise a dark or black putty will be pressed between the coloured pieces to block the white light and simulate the lead strips. At all stages the value of the dark framework must be considered as an integral part of the design. Choose one piece of a contrasting colour and attempt to make it important by isolating it with an area of the opposing colour which could eventually be black, and not necessarily central to the design.

A great understanding of the vibrant colour qualities can be gained by carrying out a number of these basic exercises.

Incidentally this method of working on a sheet of plate glass can be used for permanently fixed windows providing a sufficiently strong adhesive such as New Bostik Number 1 or Araldite is employed. Further examples of basic exercises will be seen on later pages.

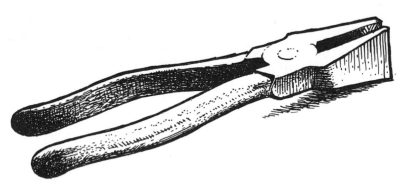

2 Grozing pliers.

TOOLS OF THE CRAFT

Having become acquainted with the beauty of coloured light through the medium of glass we can now move on to learn the methods employed by the early schools of craftsmen.

Certain items of equipment are necessary even if one is working on a limited budget.

Apart from the glass cutter which you have already been using in the initial exercise, you will need the following—

Grozing Pliers (Illustration 2). These are for the final trimming of pieces of glass and stretching of lead, besides other uses with which you will become familiar through practice.

A Lathekin (Illustrations 3–5). This implement cannot be bought, but has to be made from a piece of hardwood, approximately 7 by $1\frac{1}{4}$ inches by $\frac{1}{2}$ an inch, cut and sandpapered into shape. The lathekin is used in the main to open the edges of the leads and to eliminate any damage or wrinkles caused in storage or transit. It is also used to press the leads home into tight curves when assembling your panels of coloured glass.

3 A lathekin.

A Lead Stretcher (Illustration 6). For exact work this is an essential tool, though a small engineer's vice can be made use of to start with.

A Stopping Knife (Illustrations 7–8). This is a useful tool that can be made from an oyster knife and be converted into a form of hammer. Small nails are necessary in the making of a stained glass

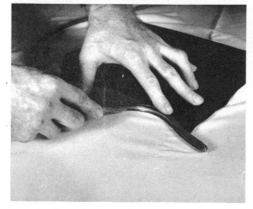 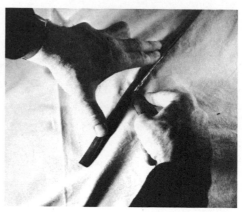

4 Pressing the lead into a curve.   **5** Opening the lead.

6 Using a lead stretcher.

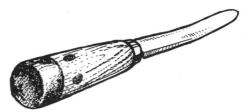

7 A stopping knife.

window, and a suitable form of hammer is required to knock them in. To make the hammer knife, first saw off about three-quarters of an inch from the handle. Now, using a $\frac{3}{16}$- or $\frac{1}{4}$-inch drill, bore a hole down the centre of the handle for about $1\frac{1}{4}$ inches and then bore two further holes half an inch from the end of the handle, and at right angles to each other, also bisecting the vertical hole. Then wrap a $2\frac{1}{2}$-inch strip of brown paper firmly around the handle leaving 1 inch projecting above the top.

Using a small steel ladle or an old tablespoon, melt some pieces of scrap lead over a gas-ring. A scum of foreign matter that rises

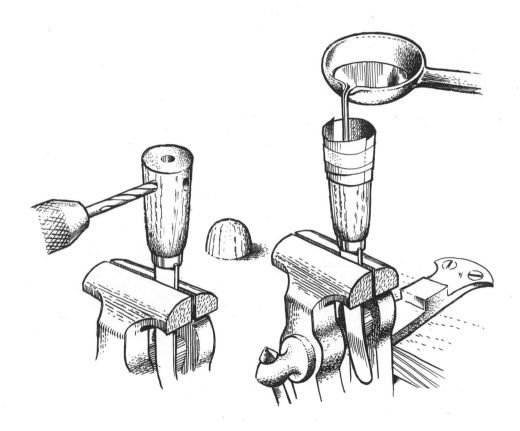

8 Making a stopping knife.

from dirty lead will appear floating on top of the ladle—this should be removed with a strip of wood or a knife blade. The melted lead should now be poured into the brown paper cylinder projecting from the end of the oyster knife handle. The molten lead will initially flow into all the holes that have been bored, thereby "locking" the hammer-head (when it is made) quite securely, whilst the remainder of the lead will form the hammer-head in the brown paper mould. The blade of the knife itself will be found useful for opening up leads that have become "bruised" or damaged in transit, and a number of other odd jobs that can arise.

A Cutting Knife (Illustrations 9–10). This is a most important tool in the kit as it is the only suitable means of cutting the leads to build up a jigsaw of coloured glass. The knife can be made from a stripping-knife obtained from a hardwear shop or decorators. This knife should be placed firmly between the jaws of a metal vice leaving approximately $1\frac{1}{2}$ inches below the top edge of the vice. With a few deliberate blows from a hammer, knock off the length of blade left projecting. The now shortened blade must be carefully sharpened to a keen edge.

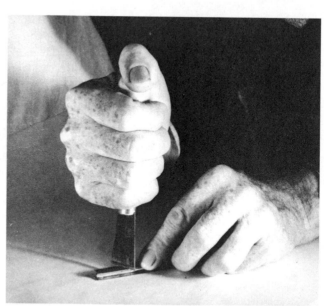

9 A cutting knife.

10 Using a cutting knife.

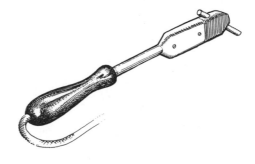

11 Nails and wood chocks.   **12** Electric soldering iron.

Nails and Chocks (Illustration 11). Round-headed 1½-inch nails are needed; also required are pieces of hardboard or plywood about 1 by ¾ by 3/16 of an inch for chocks.

An Electric Soldering Iron (Illustration 12). This should preferably be a model with a replaceable pencil bit. The working end of the bit should be filed flat and slightly domed before "tinning" ready for use.

Tinning is carried out in the following manner. Procure a spotlessly clean tin lid (the bottom end of a tin is normally clean and dust free). Upon this place a dab of Fluxite or powdered resin.

Allow the iron to reach maximum heat, then by holding a stick of solder in one hand, melt off a blob of solder into the spot of Fluxite or resin, meanwhile rubbing the end of the iron backwards and forwards through the pool of solder. When properly tinned the end of the bit should be completely covered and shining with solder.

Tallow Sticks. These are used as a flux when soldering the cut lengths of lead together.

Palette Knife (Illustration 13). This is necessary when mixing or grinding the glass-paint on a sheet of 24-ounce or ¼-plate glass. The blade should be 6 or 8 inches long.

Painting Oxides. Soft Tracing—for lining details. Geet—for toning and shading.

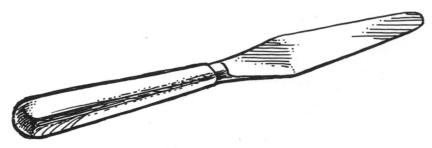

13 A palette knife.

Gum Arabic. This can be obtained in bottles or bought much cheaper from your local chemist in lump form. The lump gum arabic can be put to soak and liquefy in a jam jar containing water. The correct consistency is of thin syrup.

Electric Kiln (Illustrations 14–15). This is the most important tool of all. Through misuse, good work can be ruined, so it is most essential to exercise care in timing firings. Although special glass-firing kilns can be had for a price, front-opening electric pottery kilns can be used quite happily in conjunction with special firing

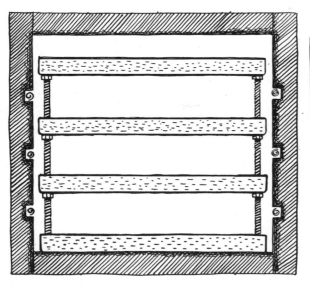

14 Cross-section of a kiln, showing the position of firing trays.

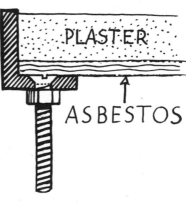

15 Section detail of firing tray.

trays. One particular kiln of this type, with internal measurements 9 by 9 by 12 inches deep, and three elements, is particularly suitable, although this method can be used with any "school-sized" kiln.

Presuming the firing chamber to be the former size, eight trays can be made (two sets of four), from $\frac{1}{2}$- by $\frac{3}{4}$-inch angle iron and heat-resisting asbestos. External measurements of the angle-iron frames should be no more than $8\frac{1}{2}$ by $11\frac{1}{2}$ inches to permit easy placing and removal of trays. The bottom tray, as can be seen in Illustration 14, stands on the floor of the kiln and those above are stacked at convenient positions midway between the electrical elements. The "legs" of the top three trays are made from $\frac{1}{4}$-inch thick countersunk bolts of suitable length, placed about $1\frac{3}{4}$ inches from each corner on the longer sides of each tray. After this operation place a sheet of heat-resisting asbestos into the well of the angle-iron frame to complete the first set of firing trays.

Before any painted glass can be fired, powdered whiting or plaster of Paris must be used to fill the tray up to the top edge. This must then be firmly pressed down to give a smooth flat surface on which the pieces of painted glass will be placed ready for firing.

Tray-Lifter (Illustration 16). To facilitate placing and removal of trays to and from the kiln an implement which is strong and safe to handle must be used. A suitable lifter can be made from mild steel, a handle being welded into place.

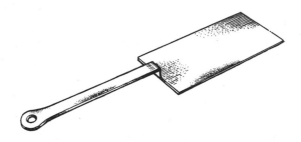

16 Tray lifter.

PROCEDURE

With the previously described tools and equipment, you are ready to construct your first stained glass window by the traditional methods of using glass and lead strips. When large ecclesiastical windows are designed it is usual to work to a scale of 1 inch to the foot, but where the student requires to make a panel about 12 by 18 inches, a $\frac{1}{4}$ scale is quite suitable. This provides an exercise in enlarging, possibly by using the "squaring up" method.

Subjects for initial designs may be suggested, symbolism from heraldic devices, monsters, animals, fish, birds and so on, as may be found on coats of arms. Redesigning from illustrations of heraldry to suit the medium of glass can be rewarding and informative, in that coats of arms require to adhere to a set range of colours as laid down by the Royal College of Heralds. Further study on the subject will help broaden the students' interests, particularly as they will be making a coat of arms or shield bearing an officially recognized "charge" in an ancient though "very much alive" craft. Visits to local churches are often worthwhile when examples of heraldic glass appear in windows recording family history.

It may now be opportune to dwell upon the methods to be employed in the creation of such a panel. With the heraldic motif in mind, a choice can be made of a mythological monster, such as a gryphon—a winged beast with an eagle or vulture head.

Make an effort to fill the rectangle to create a well-balanced design before attempting to plan where the leads are to appear. First of all remember that the leads separate one colour from another and that the width of the leads should be considered when deciding upon their arrangement. For example, here the head of the creature has been drawn (it must be borne in mind that it is not practical to press leads into sharp angles and crevices so that one must obscure incidental areas when painting to allow simple shapes for cutting). First of all draw lines representing the leads around the main features of the design, extending these lines where convenient and practical to the outside edges of the panel (see Illustrations 17–19). The lines should be to scale to represent the width of $\frac{1}{4}$- or $\frac{5}{16}$-inch strips of lead.

Where possible avoid leads crossing, for this creates a weakness

17 Drawing of main features of the design.

19 Division of the design by leads.

18 Detail of Illustration 19.

in structure. Do not be afraid of breaking up the background to your monster into smaller areas; this will mean that more leads will be used in piecing your design together, giving an added richness. With further experience this point will eventually be appreciated. As a rule, windows containing large pieces of glass and therefore fewer leads, appear weak and characterless alongside a heavily-leaded window. When the leads on your scaled drawing have been decided, go over them carefully in water-proofed Indian ink. You should now be ready to colour your design with water-colours.

To simplify matters in this first exercise, decide to use two main colours—for example, the background to be a mixture of greens

20 Cutline for armorial window.

21 Cartoon for armorial window in Bideford Parish Church (N. Devon).

and the monster in various tints and tones of purple. If you try to avoid placing two pieces of the same colour alongside each other you will go a long way towards capturing that mosaic quality which will make your panel look "glassy". When the colouring has been completed you are ready to enlarge your design to its full size—or as they say in the profession—to draw the cartoon. As in the case of large church windows with complicated traceries, this is a most important job.

When executing a rectangular window one must be certain that all corners are strictly square. Draw your rectangle to the required size, then draw another within and parallel to it only $\frac{1}{2}$ inch smaller all round. This represents a framework or outside lead $\frac{1}{2}$ inch wide. By squaring up your sketch design you should find the task of

22 Evangelist window, St. Luke,
by Michael Maybee.

23 The Prisoners
by Michael Maybee.

enlarging fairly simple if you exert a reasonable amount of care. Using a water-colour brush, paint all your lines in black ink $\frac{1}{4}$ or $\frac{5}{16}$ inch wide, thereby representing the leads you intend to use. You can now continue to outline your full-size design with a dark opaque colour such as Vandyke Brown and fill in all the areas to complete the silhouette of your subject. With a 3B pencil you can add shading and tone where you require it.

CUTTING

A cutting plan, professionally known as the "cutline", must now be prepared before you go any further. Although the ideal is to use linen tracing cloth the expense involved may prohibit its use; therefore, with a certain amount of care, strong tracing paper or even grease-proof paper can be used as good substitutes. Take a piece of tracing material at least 1 inch larger all round than your cartoon and pin it firmly down to your drawing board over the cartoon. With a number 2 brush paint a line just over $\frac{1}{16}$ inch thick along the centre of all the lead lines which of course should be visible through the tracing paper. This line can be readily drawn with a sharp 3B pencil or ball-pen. The important point about this operation is that the line should be drawn as accurately and as constant as possible

24 Cutline for a panel of the west window in
St. Paul's Parish Church, Barnstable.

25 Cartoon for a tracery light.

26 Cartoon of a panel of the west window, St. Sidwell's Church, Exeter.

27 Cartoon for a panel of the west window in St. Paul's Parish Church, Barnstable.

in thickness, for it represents the core or heart of the lead, which is always $\frac{1}{16}$ inch thick irrespective of how wide the leads are. Do not forget to draw this line also along the centre of the $\frac{1}{2}$-inch leads making the framework of your cartoon.

The important preliminaries being completed, the actual cutting of the pieces of glass to make the "jig-saw puzzle" can be started. It will be appreciated that the areas in between your network of black lines represent the exact sizes of your pieces of glass. The

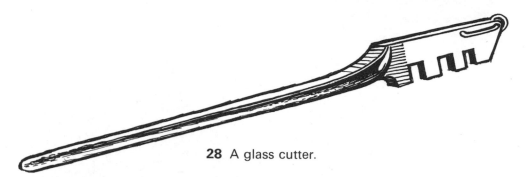

28 A glass cutter.

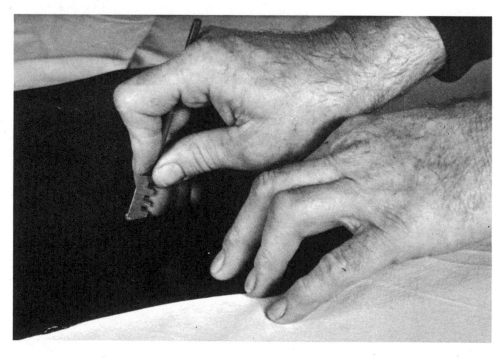

29 Holding the cutter and the glass.

22

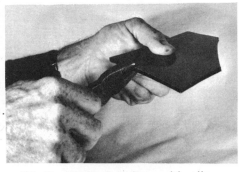

30 Tapping underneath the cut prior to breaking.

31 Breaking the glass with pliers.

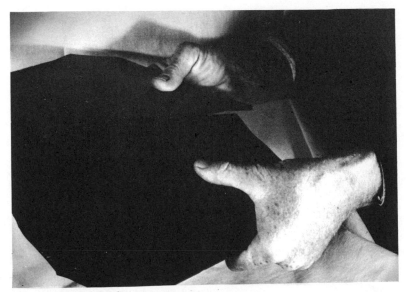

32 Removing the sharp edges by scraping one against the other.

small coloured design will help to guide you in your choice of colour for individual shapes, so you can now proceed to select the glass.

Avoid waste if possible by using pieces slightly larger in area than the piece you intend to cut. Place it on the cutline and with the glass-cutter (Illustration 28) held correctly and firmly between the first and second fingers (Illustration 29) follow the inside edge of the line with the edge of the small steel cutting wheel. Always commence your cut from the edge of the piece of glass and continue along the intended line to the farther edge. Hold the glass in

33 Panel by Paul Blaney.

34 King Solomon by Anthony Jarman.

your left hand and tap on the underside of the line made by the cutting wheel, with the slotted edge of your glass-cutter (Illustration 30). This encourages correct breakage. Now take up the piece of glass in both hands and with a firm upward pressure snap the glass clean in two. Sometimes of course there may be insufficient space to grip with the fingers in which case the flat-nosed pliers should be used (Illustration 31). As a safety measure to guard against cutting the hands, always scrape one cut edge against the other immediately after completing a cut (Illustration 32).

If finances will not run to the expense of making a light-table other methods can be employed. The simplest is to make a template from the cutline, just slightly smaller than the shape to cut. All you have to do is to place the template down on the piece of glass and cut round the edges.

By observing the thickness of some of the coloured sheets of glass a thin skin or veneer of colour fused to a white or lighter-coloured glass may be noticed. This is created in the process of blowing the glass during its manufacture. This is called "Flashed Glass". Sheets that are of one colour throughout are called "Pot" colours. Cut flashed glass with the flash on the underside or you will find difficulty in cutting. As each piece is cut tick off the respective shape on your cutline and place it in position on the cartoon.

The correct method of using the cutter is to draw the wheel towards you when cutting although the beginner may be able to execute more accurate cutting by the reverse method. When the piece required has been cut it should be checked on the cutline to ensure that it is a perfect fit. Slight irregularities can be removed by careful "nibbling" with the grozing pliers. All pieces of glass forming your design must be checked on the cutline, for it is better at this stage to be correct than to risk flaking and breakage by grozing after painting and firing. You will find it easy to see the lines of the cutline through light-coloured glass, but when darker colours require cutting you will find it impossible to see through the glass when it is laid flat upon the cutting bench. To overcome this problem you will have to construct a workshop table (as seen in Illustration 1 on page 5) with a sheet of plate glass fixed on the top and a sheet of mirror positioned beneath it, which can be adjusted to reflect the light upwards. Small tube lights can be fixed beneath the plate glass.

PAINTING

With all the glass cut you can now look ahead to the exciting processes of painting and firing. First the paint must be prepared. On a piece of plain glass about 12 inches square tip a heaped dessert spoon of soft tracing powder. Add a small amount of water and a drop of prepared gum arabic, then with a muller (Illustration 35), palette knife or even a well-worn steel table knife, grind your mixture well until it is perfectly smooth. As alternative mediums, milk, sugary water, or even beer may be used for preparing the glass. paint. The longer the grinding the finer the result of the painted line. The ordinary type of water-colour paint brush will not do for glass painting. There is no cheap substitute, and a little money spent on a dozen or so brushes specially made for the job will be well worth the expense. Glass paint does not flow as easily as water colours; therefore the brush head has to be larger and longer to hold a workable amount of the mixture and to be of stronger hair to carry the extra weight without drooping. To facilitate control when painting a hand-rest can be very helpful (Illustration 36). A strip of 2- by $\frac{1}{2}$-inch batten nailed across two blocks of wood about $1\frac{1}{2}$ inches high at a convenient width of 14 to 16 inches will suffice.

Place the cartoon on a flat desk or table top at a suitable working height, then select a few pieces of glass requiring to be painted. It is essential to ensure that the surface is free of dirt and grease before painting; to achieve this, dab a spot of glass paint on to the surface then with a damp rag rub hard until it is perfectly clean.

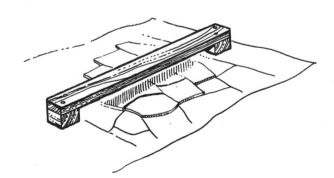

35 A glass muller. **36** A hand-rest for tracing.

Carefully place your pieces of glass in their respective positions on the cartoon and with the hand-rest spanning the working area, load your brush with paint and proceed to trace the outline and details which you can see through the glass. When this has been done place them safely on one side and continue to complete all the tracing. Remember to use the light-table for painting when tracing on dark-coloured glass.

With the painting completed the stage has been reached for the first firing. To save expense, in schools or clubs, it is often sensible to wait until a number of people are at the same stage with their designs when all the work can be fired together.

FIRING

Presuming the firing trays have been prepared and the loose plaster of Paris filling has been carefully smoothed down with a small trowel or palette knife, the painted glass can be placed in position for firing. When doing this it is best to lay out the largest pieces first and then to fill in the gaps with smaller pieces. As some glasses are hard and others comparatively soft (this will be discovered with experience), try to remember when loading the trays to place the hard pieces in the hottest part of the kiln. The front of the kiln is usually the coolest area.

When the trays have been loaded, place them in position in the firing chamber using the tray-lifter (Illustration 16). Finally check the kiln door to see if it will close properly, then switch on the current. Leave the peephole bung open and fire at minimum temperature for the first twenty minutes.

A worthwhile principle to remember is to fire slowly and cool gradually. Increase the temperature slowly after replacing the bung and in about another twenty minutes you will observe through the peephole that the kiln interior is beginning to get red and glowing. As the firing process is to fuse the paint to the surface of the glass, it is of course necessary to increase the heat gradually until the surface starts to melt. At first it is difficult to assess the right moment when this takes place. Until fully confident, carefully check the time of switching on and note the increase in temperature. It is possible when using this type of kiln to open the door slightly to more easily observe the surfaces of the pieces of glass on the trays.

It is so easy to overfire. Take warning and do not take any risks that might spoil a lot of hard work. In the beginning it is better to underfire than to overfire. When the paint appears to have a slight sheen denoting that it has fluxed the firing should be complete. Switch off, remove the bung, and in ten minutes or so open the door slightly. In fifteen minutes it should be possible, while exercising care, to remove the trays one by one with the tray-lifter. They can be stood on top of the kiln where the atmosphere is warm, to allow the pieces of glass to cool gradually and to become sufficiently cool to handle.

Meanwhile the kiln door is closed to conserve what heat remains and the other set of trays are prepared for firing. When these are ready you will find it quite safe to place them in the warm kiln. Wait for ten minutes or so then start to increase the kiln temperature once again. As the second batch of trays is being placed in the already heated kiln, the fluxing temperature will be reached somewhat sooner than the first batch.

To remove the fairly warm pieces of glass from the cooling trays, use a warm palette knife blade and lift them off on to a warm surface —avoid placing warm glass on to a cold metal surface. Providing all the tracing lines of the pieces of glass have fired well it will be possible to add tone and shading to the panel to give it character.

FURTHER PAINTING PROCESSES

First of all place a sheet of glass completely over the cutline and then by attaching three or four small blobs of Plasticene on the underside edges of the pieces of coloured glass, press them down in their respective positions over the cutline. When all the pieces of glass have been fixed in place raise the sheet of plate glass in both hands and hold it up to the light. This is the first moment for an accurate critical appraisal of the panel. However, there is still much to be done.

A form of easel (Illustration 37), probably on a bench in front of the window, should be on hand to permit the applying of the "matt". This is more or less a wash of glass paint applied with a sable-mop brush and then smoothed evenly with a badger-hair brush (Illustration 38). The matt surface can also be stippled before it dries with the end part of the badger brush. If the matt is applied too

37 A bench-type easel.

heavily it will tend to hide the outline and details. Even so, by stippling the surface a luminosity is created which reveals the outline more clearly.

When the surface has dried completely some old hog-hair brushes of various sizes will be needed (Illustration 38). With these pick out the highlights and add form to the design. Practise controlling graduated tones and see what sparkle can be added by removing spots and lines with a sharpened piece of wood— usually the end of an old brush or penholder; an old-fashioned metal gramophone needle pushed firmly with a pair of pliers into another brush handle, is also a useful tool to have (Illustration 38). Try out interesting textures on the background pieces with the various "tools" and see what happens when the matt surface is rubbed with the end of a finger. It is all very exciting and mistakes can easily be wiped off and other attempts made before firing. The same principles apply when preparations are made to fire the glass for the second time.

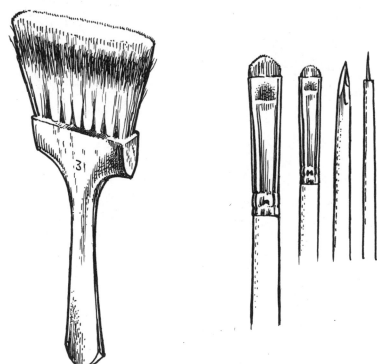

38 A badger-hair brush, old hog-hair brushes, a sharpened piece of wood, and a needle point.

39 Musical Instrument panel by Neil Pritchard.

40 Copy by the Author of a King from Winchester Cathedral.
The original is now in the Victoria and Albert Museum.

LEADING

When the painting has been completed and fired the glass is ready for "leading up". This must be done on the glazing bench, a heavy work table which can withstand a lot of punishment. Lay out the cutline, quite smooth and flat on the bench, and fix it down with drawing pins or Sellotape. A length of batten about 1½ inches wide is then placed along one side of the cutline parallel to the edge. Select whatever lead it is intended to use as a border lead, place this against the wood strip and, by taking a piece of glass adjacent to the edge, adjust its position in conjunction with the lead and wood strip until it corresponds with the cutline. Do the same at the other end and when certain that it is correct, nail home the wood strip firmly on to the glazing bench. With a second strip of wood, place it at right angles and carry out the same procedure as before (Illustration 41). Check the angle with a set square. It is worth the

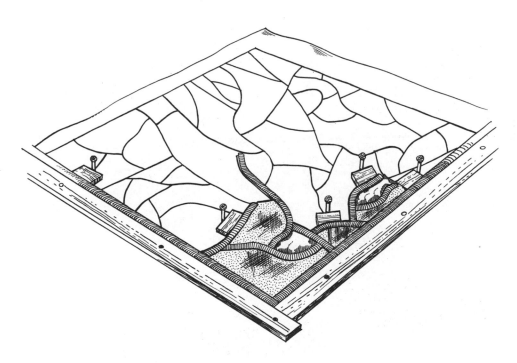

41 Leading a panel on the glazing bench.

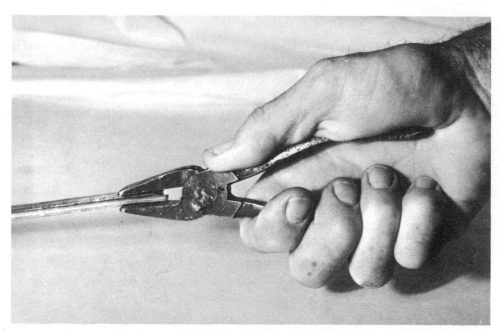

42 Stretching the lead (see Illustration 6).

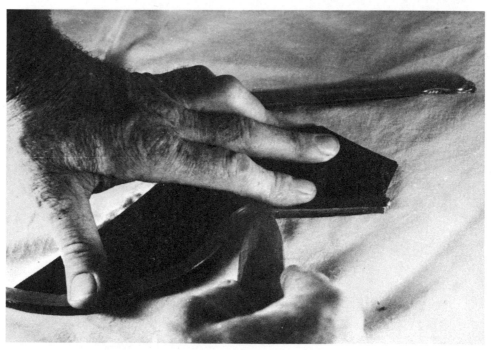

43 Using a lathekin (see Illustrations 3–5).

effort to make sure that these important preliminaries are correct before continuing.

With both wood strips nailed down, next take a length or "calme" of lead and stretch it. This is done by fastening one end in a lead stretcher (Illustration 6) or engineer's vice and with the other end firmly held in a pair of grozing pliers give it a sharp tug (Illustration 42). Do not over-stretch. Now lay the lead on the bench and run the lathekin up and down the core between the flanges of the lead to eliminate any irregularities (Illustration 43). Using the cutting knife, now cut lengths to lay alongside the strips of wood to form the outside lead of your panel. Using small chocks of wood and nails, hold these in position by tucking them between the flanges of the lead (Illustration 41).

The first piece of glass to be fitted will of course be that which fits into the corner. Press it home and a little gentle persuasion can be exercised with the head of your stopping knife. It should coincide correctly with the *inside* edge of the cutline. If it appears to be too big, use the grozing pliers to "nibble" it to the correct size. Now proceed to cut your short pieces of lead and add to your jigsaw building up all the time and firmly tapping home the glass with the stopping knife to correspond accurately with the cutline.

Note the varying thicknesses of the pieces of glass and choose the correct sized leads to fit (Illustration 44). As the work progresses it is advisable to hold the pieces of glass in position with one of the chocks of wood and a nail tapped alongside into the bench.

When the leading of all the small pieces is completed, the next stage is to apply the outside or border lead. Check all the outside edges of the glass and then with the lead cut to size and opened with the lathekin, coax it into position. A 12-inch ruler is handy for flanges and giving a few firm taps with the stopping knife. Hold the ruler in position with two or three nails then continue to complete the panel by adding the final strip of border lead.

The next operation is to solder all the joints (Illustration 46). Clean lead is an absolute essential to good soldering. An effective method of cleaning the joints should be used; they may be either scraped with a knife blade, rubbed with a piece of emery cloth or a small scratch card may be used. A flux is then applied to each joint. This is done by a light dab from a tallow candle. While this is being done your soldering iron can be switched on and gaining heat.

Take a strip of solder in the left hand and the soldering iron in the right (providing of course that you are normally right-handed). The end of the strip of solder is touched by the copper bit of the iron and it will collect a small drop of molten solder. The soldering iron is now

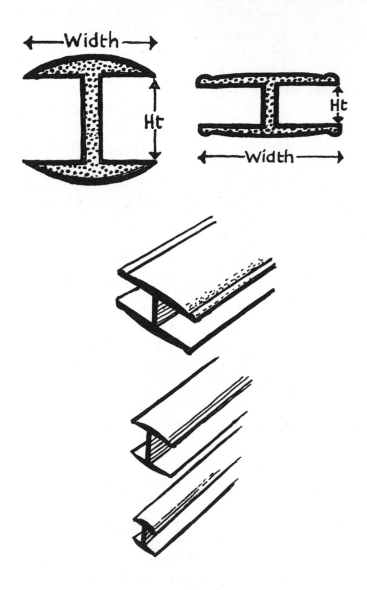

44 Choose correct sizes of leads.

45 Cross section of a panel showing the leads.

lowered to allow the blob of solder to touch the joint when it will immediately flow evenly over the joint. Providing the copper bit is hot enough there is no need to press down on the joint. When one side is completed carefully check to make sure that no joints have been missed, and then turn the panel over and continue the process on the other side.

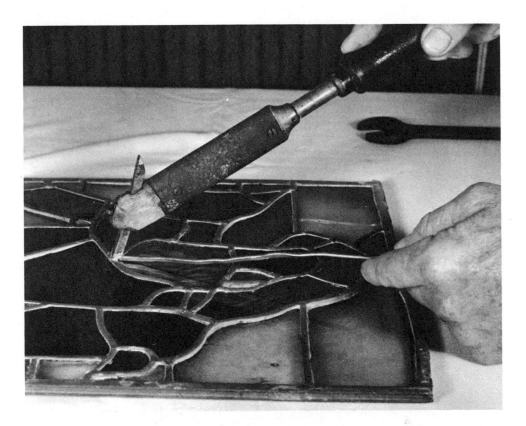

46 Soldering a joint.

CEMENTING

To ensure a weather-proof and watertight window a special mixture of cement must be applied to both sides. The ingredients for this are as follows: 4 or 5 parts of powdered whiting, 4 parts of plaster of Paris, 2 parts of driers, 1 part of lamp black or black paint, to which is added boiled linseed oil and a little turpentine, mixing to achieve a consistency not unlike rice pudding.

Lay the panel on the bench and simply ladle a quantity on to the surface then with a small old scrubbing brush push it around into all the crevices. Do this job thoroughly then sprinkle some powdered whiting lightly over the surface and scrub once again preferably with another brush which is not clogged with cement. Turn the panel over and proceed to cement the other side. After a final trim up round the edges of the leads with a pointed stick and a polish with a dry piece of rag, the first stained glass window is complete.

EXPERIMENTS IN OTHER METHODS

On a piece of plain glass create an abstract design with odd pieces of coloured glass similar to the method quoted in the Introduction. After carefully selecting your pieces, lightly smear the underside with gum and place them down in position, leaving no less than $\frac{1}{2}$ an inch between them. You now prepare some pottery clay, not too soft, which should be rolled with a rolling pin to an even thickness about 1 inch thick. Using a sharp knife, carefully cut out clay shapes similar to your pieces of glass but $\frac{1}{8}$ inch less all round. This can be easily achieved by simply taking one piece of glass at a time, placing it on the clay, lightly scoring a line around it and then cutting through the clay with a vertical cut approximately $\frac{1}{8}$ inch within the scored line. As each piece of glass is returned to its original position place the corresponding lumps of clay centrally on each piece. Make certain the clay adheres to the surface of the glass by lightly wetting the underside.

You are now almost ready to cast the cement. First place some strips of wood approximately 2 inches by $\frac{1}{2}$ an inch around the edge

47 Preparing a sketch with the pieces of glass shown in white will indicate the effect of light coming through the completed panel.

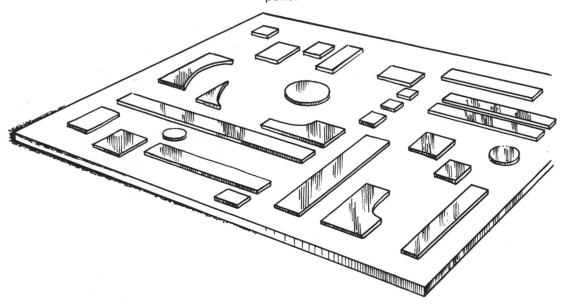

48 Laying out the pieces of glass on the foundation board.

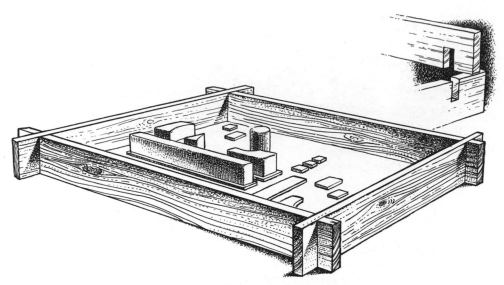

49 Clay shapes.

50 Cement cast panels creating wall area.

42

of the glass in the manner shown. Mix the cement and sand in the proportion of 1 cement to 3 of sand and then carefully pour and trowel into position without disturbing the clay, to a regular depth of $\frac{1}{2}$ an inch. Leave for 30 minutes and then cut some lengths of galvanized iron wire which should be placed centrally in the cement areas between the pieces of glass. This operation is followed by pouring in the remaining cement mix to complete the casting. Allow to set and remove the clay after 24 hours. Any irregularities within the walls of the openings can be patched with some spare cement and a small palette knife. The resulting panel can be most satisfying. By this method, interesting wall areas can be created. (Instead of using cement one can of course use plaster of Paris.) (Illustration 50.)

COLOURED TISSUES

Brightly coloured tissue paper can provide useful exercises. Cut shapes pasted down on to white tissue, sometimes overlapping and designed to give over-printing effects—strips of black paper representing the leads are then pasted down separating each individually coloured shape. This same exercise can be performed using coloured Cellophane, though some difficulty may be found in discovering the most suitable adhesive. Cowgum or clear Bostik used sparingly are reasonably successful. Areas of printed colour cut from magazine covers and illustrations can be stuck down on to black paper in a manner reminiscent of stained glass.

A commodity named Permaled, which is retailed in a flat lead strip, offers interesting possibilities (Illustration 51). Pieces of coloured Cellophane are placed down on a sheet of clear 18-ounce glass which lies over a piece of cartridge paper bearing the design. The Cellophane areas should be lightly tacked down to prevent movement before placing another sheet of glass of the same dimensions on top, thereby creating a sandwich. The edges can be held together with strips of Sellotape, passe-partout, or insulation tape. You are now ready to apply the Permaled strip. It comes in rolls of four strips wide, each of which can be easily separated from the

51 Permaled.

other. (A special tin of adhesive is supplied with the Permaled.) The strips can be cut to size with a knife or scissors and stuck down on to the glass over the coloured Cellophane separating the different areas of colour (Illustration 54).

Collage in imitation of stained glass can be practised with areas of printed colour cut from old magazine covers and illustrations, pasted down on to black paper (Illustration 52).

GLASS CONSTRUCTIONS

Fascinating constructions can be built with rectangular pieces of glass (Illustration 53). Choose a base of clear glass, preferably $\frac{1}{4}$ plate, about 8 by 6 inches, and on this carefully fix rectangles of coloured glass, of similar width, edgewise with clear Bostik or Araldite, upon which level platforms of glass can be similarly fixed. For perfect adhesion the pieces of glass must be cut well, that is, snapped clean after scoring the surface with the glass cutter. By building up story upon story with a variety of different-coloured rectangles you can achieve a very colourful tower. The effect can be vividly enhanced by placing the completed structure over a light box.

52 A collage imitation of stained glass, using printed coloured paper cut from magazines and stuck down on to black paper.

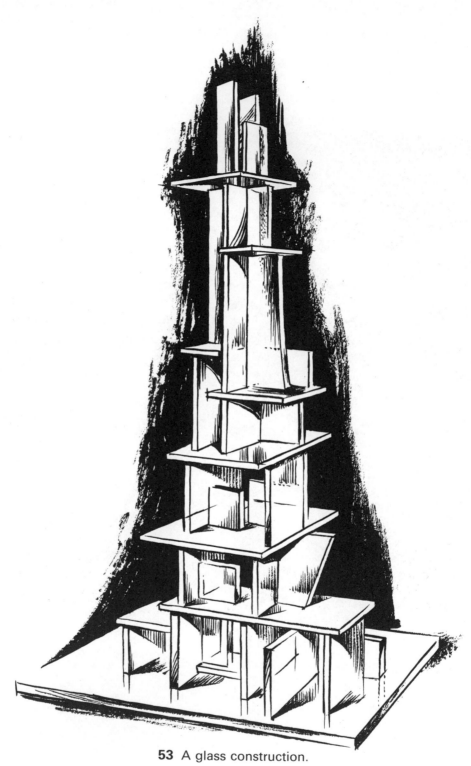

53 A glass construction.

MATERIAL SUPPLIERS

Information as to instruction and careers in the craft of stained glass can be obtained by contacting the nearest art school. The firms listed below can be contacted for materials and they will send catalogues on receipt of your name and address.

James Hetley & Co. Ltd, Beresford Avenue, Wembley, Middlesex. Suppliers of glass, paint, cutting knives, soldering irons, lead-stretchers etc.

Bruntons Ltd, 5 Miles Street, London S.W.8.
Suppliers of window lead, solder etc.
Builders' merchants for plaster of Paris, and heat-resisting asbestos.
Decorators for boiled linseed oil and turpentine.

James Hetley & Co. Ltd, Beresford Avenue, Wembley, Middlesex. Suppliers of boxed lots of glass pieces very suitable for school work, from about two shillings and sixpence a pound.